PATHFINDERS IN EXPLORATION

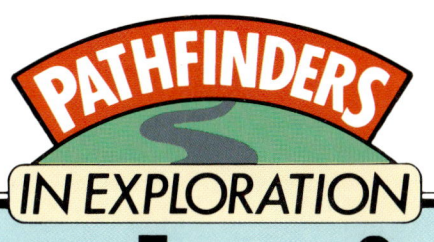

Exploring the Poles

EDITORIAL PLANNING
AMR

MACMILLAN

910 ARC

© Macmillan Education Ltd 1987

All rights reserved. No reproduction, copy or transmission of this publication may be made without written permission.

No paragraph of this publication may be reproduced, copied or transmitted save with written permission or in accordance with the provisions of the Copyright Act 1956 (as amended), or under the terms of any licence permitting limited copying issued by the Copyright Licensing Agency, 33 – 4 Alfred Place, London WC1E 7DP.

Any person who does any unauthorised act in relation to this publication may be liable to criminal prosecution and civil claims for damages.

First published 1987

Published by
MACMILLAN EDUCATION LTD
Houndmills, Basingstoke, Hampshire RG21 2XS
and London
Companies and representatives
throughout the world

Authors: Derek Cullen and John Murray-Robertson

Designed and typeset by The Pen and Ink Book Company Ltd, London

Illustrated by Gecko Ltd

Picture research by Faith Perkins

Printed in Hong Kong

British Library Cataloguing in Publication Data

Exploring the poles. – (Pathfinders in exploration).
1. Polar regions – Exploration – Juvenile literature
I. Series
919.9′04   TL793

ISBN 0-333-43948-1
ISBN 0-333-43953-8 Series

Photographic Credits

t=top b=bottom l=left r=right

The author and publishers wish to acknowledge, with thanks, the following photographic sources: 12 Aspect Picture Library, London; 12-13, 15*t*, 16*b*, 20, 34*r* BBC Hulton Picture Library, London; 19*r*, 25*t* Bettmann Archive, New York; 9*t* Bodleian Library, Oxford; 36-37 The Cavalry and Guards Club, London; 7*r*, 19*l*, 22 Bruce Coleman (UK); 9*b*, 25*b*, 40 Mary Evans Picture Library, London; 27, 43*t*, 43*b* Ranulph Fiennes; 13, 14-15, 16*t* Fram Museum, Oslo; 7*l* Robert Harding Picture Library, London; 21*b* Historical Newspaper Service, London; 26-27 (Weidenfeld Archive) Illustrated London News; 17 Knudsens fotosenter, Oslo; 10-11 (photographs by Michael Holford), 23*r* (Weidenfeld Archive) National Maritime Museum, London; 38 Peter Newark's Historical Pictures; 33 title page, Picturepoint(UK); 30, 32, 33*t*, 35, 37*t* Popperfoto, London; 21*t* (Weidenfeld Archive), 39*l* Royal Geographical Society, London; 31 (Weidenfeld Archive) Scott Polar Research Institute, Cambridge; contents page, 4, 5, 23*l*, 26, 28, 29, 34*l*, 37*b*, 41*t*, 41*b* John Topham Picture Library (UK); 42 Trans-Antarctic Expedition

Cover photograph courtesy of Picturepoint (UK)

The publishers have made every effort to trace the copyright holders, but if they have inadvertently overlooked any, they will be pleased to make the necessary arrangement at the first opportunity.

Note to the reader
In this book there are some words in the text which are printed in **bold** type. This shows that the word is listed in the glossary on page 46. The glossary gives a brief explanation of words which may be new to you.

Contents

Introduction	4	Shackleton alone	28
Where are the Poles?	6	The race to the South Pole	30
The Northwest Passage	8	Amundsen arrives	32
The expedition that disappeared	10	Struggle and success	34
The search for the North Pole	12	Scott's last journey	36
Nansen and the *Fram*	14	More challenges in the Antarctic	38
The Northwest Passage at last	16	Flying in polar regions	40
The US and the North Pole	18	New challenges	42
First at the North Pole?	20		
Antarctica	22	Quiz	44
The first sight of Antarctica	24	Glossary	46
The two rivals	26	Index	48

Pathfinders

Introduction

The North Pole is the name given to the point in the world which is the furthest north. The South Pole is the point furthest south. The poles are the coldest places on Earth. These **polar regions**, as they are called, are always covered with ice. It is very hard to travel there because it is so cold. Until a number of years ago, nobody had reached the North or the South Pole. This book describes the journeys in the polar regions and the people who risked their lives there.

▼ An explorer in the Arctic during the Transglobe Expedition. Ranulph Fiennes and Charles Burton reached the North Pole on 11 April 1982. Later, they used satellite photographs to help them plan their route through the melting pack ice.

North and south

The polar region in the north is called the **Arctic** and the polar region in the south is called the **Antarctic**. In the winter, it is always dark in the polar regions because the sun never rises. In the Arctic, it is midwinter in January, while in the Antarctic it is midwinter in June. Both regions are always very cold and covered with ice, but they are even colder in the winter.

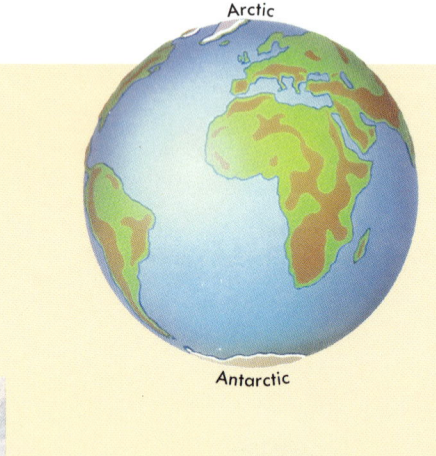

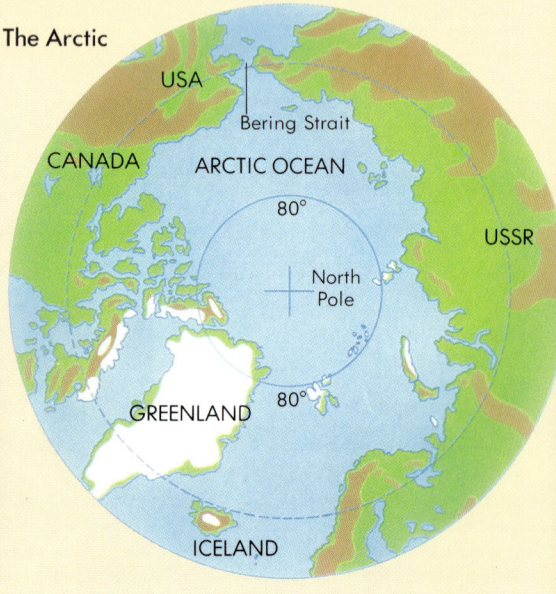

Introduction

In other ways, the North and South Poles are not the same. The Arctic is an ocean with land all around it. The Antarctic is a land with sea all around it. The Arctic Ocean is covered with thick ice which **drifts** about. Antarctica is very large. It is the size of Europe and the United States put together. It covers about one-tenth of the surface of the Earth. It is even colder there than in the Arctic. No one except a few scientists live on this land, and there is no other land near it. The ocean around it is often frozen.

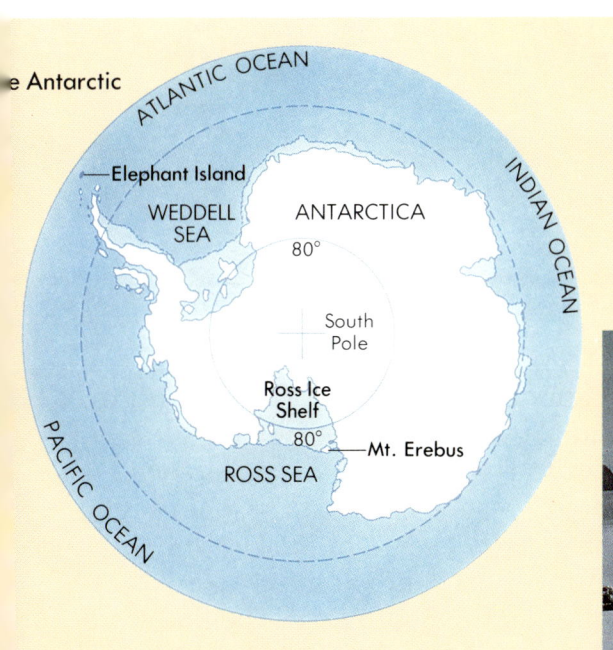

Why explore the Poles?

Why did people face such bitter cold, danger and hardship to explore the polar regions? Their journeys took a very long time, sometimes years. Most people who explored these cold regions wanted to find out what was there. They also wanted to gain honour for themselves and for their country. On their travels, they found the best **routes** and made maps. They also found out a lot that scientists wanted to know.

The people who explored the polar regions had to be strong and fit. They wanted to prove to themselves that they could face hardship and defeat it.

▼ Antarctica is the coldest, iciest and windiest place on Earth. In winter, the temperature is often −60 °C and the winds can blow up to 300 km an hour.

Pathfinders

Where are the Poles?

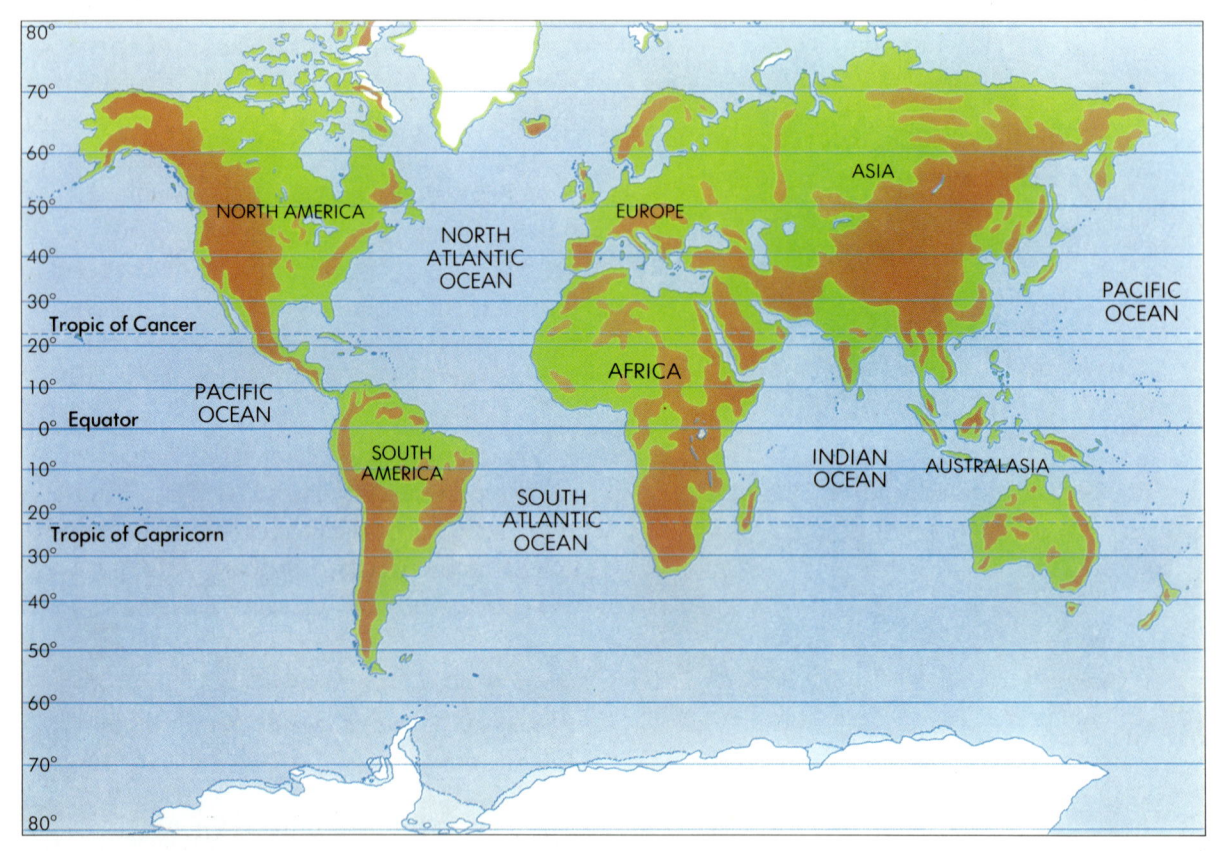

▲ The lines drawn across this map of the world are lines of latitude. They run parallel to each other. An instrument called a sextant is used to give a ship its latitude, north or south of the Equator.

We can find out how far north or south in the world a place is by using the lines drawn on maps and globes. The lines which are drawn around a globe are called lines of **latitude**. The first line is around the middle of the world and is given the number 0 **degrees**. We call this line the **Equator**. There are 90 lines, or degrees, of latitude north of the Equator, and 90 degrees south of it.

London, in Britain is about 52° north and New York, in the United States, is about 41° north. Sydney, Australia is about 34° south. The furthest north you can go is 90° north, or the North Pole. The furthest south you can go is 90° south, or the South Pole. The line of latitude which is just over 66° north is called the **Arctic Circle**. It is 2600 km from the North Pole. In the south, the line just over 66° south is 2600 km from the South Pole and is called the **Antarctic Circle**.

▶ After the spring thaw, pieces of ice float around in the Arctic Ocean. The wind can blow the ice in one direction and trap a ship.

Where are the Poles?

Finding the Poles

When people want to find out which direction is north, they look at a **compass**. The needle of a compass seems to point towards the North Pole. In fact, it is not pointing towards the North Pole, but slightly away from it. This is because the Earth is slightly angled towards the Sun as it spins around it. The compass needle points towards the **magnetic north**, not the North Pole. People have to allow for this as they go towards the North Pole, which is the true north.

The same is true in the south. The South Pole is the true south, not the **magnetic south.**

The Arctic

Inside the Arctic Circle, there is land and ocean. The Arctic is bigger in area than Europe. The North Pole is near the middle of the Arctic Ocean. It is covered with ice during the winter, but some of the ice breaks up in the summer.

The lands which surround the Arctic Ocean include the northern part of the USSR, Canada, Greenland and Alaska in the United States. In the winter, these lands are frozen. In the summer, the top soil **thaws**, but in many places the ground below is always frozen. This is called **permafrost**. This means that plants cannot put down deep roots. Only moss and small bushes can grow there.

Many animals live in these regions. There are caribou, hares, foxes, polar bears and seals. There are also small groups of people, like the Inuit and Saami, who have lived in the Arctic regions for thousands of years. Today, there are big towns there like Murmansk in the USSR and Anchorage in Alaska because coal, oil and iron have been found under the frozen ground.

▲ Some Inuit families still use husky dogs to pull their sledges. In many Arctic areas, snowmobiles are now used to carry goods.

Pathfinders

The Northwest Passage

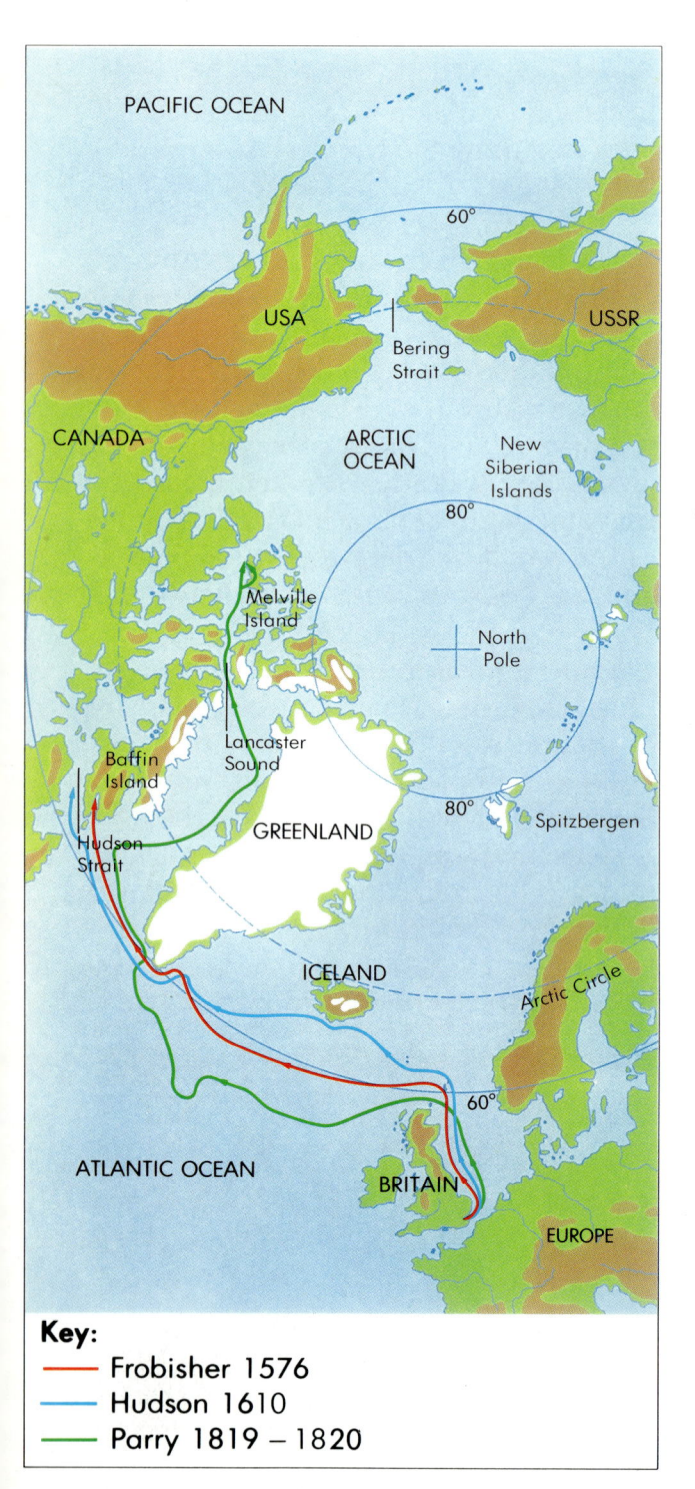

About 450 years ago, people travelled by sea from Europe to Asia. They used the route around the Cape of Good Hope, at the southern tip of Africa. It was a long journey through seas which could be very rough. As a result of this, explorers began to look for another route which they could use to reach Asia. They hoped to find a **Northwest Passage** from the Atlantic Ocean to the Pacific Ocean. Today, we know that this means sailing through the frozen Arctic Ocean north of Canada. In those days, people in Europe knew little about Canada. They did not know that it was such a big country.

The first explorers

The French were the first to look for the Northwest Passage. For a time, they thought they might find a way to Asia by going along the St Lawrence River and through the Great Lakes in North America.

In 1576, Martin Frobisher left England to search for a route. He sailed to Greenland and then to Baffin Island, near the eastern coast of Canada. He could get no further because of the frozen sea.

◀ In the 1500s, the search started for a northern sea route from the Atlantic Ocean to the Pacific Ocean. This was called the Northwest Passage. The Spanish and Portuguese merchants had already set up trade routes around the tips of South America and South Africa. The English also wanted to profit from the spice trade with Asia, or the East as it was called.

Key:
— Frobisher 1576
— Hudson 1610
— Parry 1819 – 1820

8

The Northwest Passage

▲ Martin Frobisher was sure he would find a Northwest Passage to the Pacific Ocean. He was sent by Queen Elizabeth of England to find this passage in 1576.

In 1610, Henry Hudson sailed into the wide entrance of what is now called Hudson Bay. He thought it might be the Northwest Passage, but his **crew** would go no further with him. They forced him off his ship into a small boat. He died later of cold and hunger.

In 1616, William Baffin found a route past the north of Baffin Island called Lancaster Sound. Ice forced him to turn back. He did not know that he had found the entrance to the Northwest Passage. People began to doubt there was any way through the ice, and exploration stopped for a while.

William Edward Parry

Two hundred years later, people began to look for the Northwest Passage again. A reward of £20 000 was to be given by the British government to the first person to find it.

In 1819, William Edward Parry set off on an **expedition** with two ships, the *Hecla* and the *Griper*. Parry had been in the Navy and he was a good sailor. He also knew a lot about science.

To help Parry through the large areas of **pack ice**, he sometimes tied his ship to an **iceberg**. An iceberg is a tall, floating block of ice. The iceberg smashed its way through the thinner ice as it floated. The iceberg pulled Parry's ship along behind it.

Parry got further west than any other explorer had done. He reached Melville Island, but then had to give up. The pack ice was too thick for him to go any further. When Parry and his crew arrived home, they were given £5000.

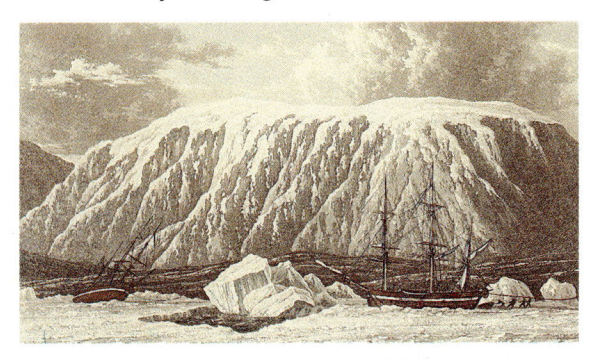

▲ Edward Parry also went to find the Northwest Passage. He sailed with two ships called the *Hecla* and the *Griper*. The ships had to spend the winter in the Arctic when they became stuck in the pack ice.

Pathfinders

The expedition that disappeared

The search for the Northwest Passage went on. In 1819, John Franklin sailed across Hudson Bay. He left his ship at the place where the Nelson River flows into the sea. From there, he went on foot with three of his crew to the Great Slave Lake. With the help of local hunters who showed him the way, Franklin moved north to the coast. Franklin walked along 880 km of the coast and saw an area which no one from Europe had seen before.

Franklin's last journey

Franklin was now a well-known man, but it was his last journey which made him most famous. In May 1845, when he was 59 years old, Franklin set off again with two ships. These ships, the *Erebus* and the *Terror*, had sailed in the icy seas before, and their crews knew a lot about sailing through pack ice. Franklin took enough food, or **supplies**, to last for three years. Two months later, in July 1845, Franklin and his ships were seen for the last time. He was at Lancaster Sound, the entrance to the Northwest Passage.

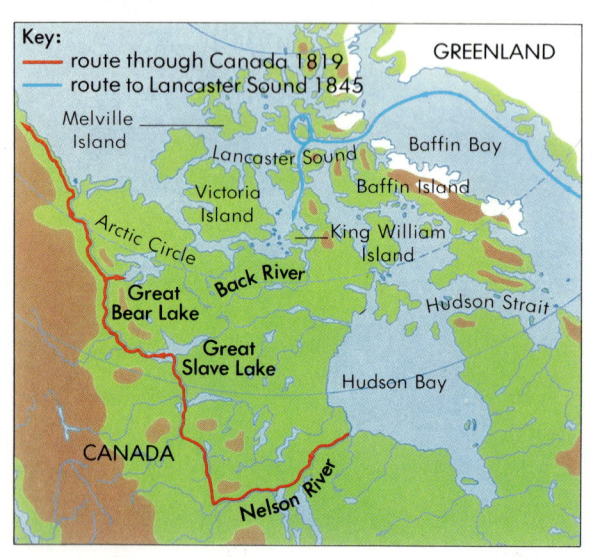

▼ The *Erebus* and the *Terror* caught in an Arctic storm. The two ships were built to survive the rough polar waters. They were able to fight their way through the pack ice without being crushed.

▲ The route John Franklin took in search of the Northwest Passage.

The expedition that disappeared

The search for Franklin

When Franklin did not return, people in Britain wanted to find out where he was. The government, and Franklin's wife, offered money to anyone who could find out what had happened to him. The first attempts were made in 1848. During the next ten years, 40 groups set off to try and find him. The first news came in 1850. One group of searchers found a storehouse which Franklin had used. Three people were buried near the storehouse, but Franklin was not one of them.

More news came in 1854. One of the searchers, Dr John Rae, heard a strange story from the local Inuit. They said they had seen 40 strangers walking south along the Back River. Their ship had been wrecked near King William Island, and they had reached the mainland in lifeboats. The Inuit had clothes and knives and forks which had come from the two ships. The 40 men had been Franklin's crew, but Dr Rae did not know if Franklin had been among them.

Franklin's wife still wanted to find out about her husband, so she bought a ship called the *Fox*. The captain headed for the Back River. In 1859, he found one of Franklin's lifeboats, and a large pile of stones. Under the stones, the captain found some notes written by Franklin's crew. The notes said that Franklin had died on 11 June 1847 on board his ship. Franklin's crew were never found.

▲ This medicine chest was found by one of the search parties looking for Franklin and his men. It contained the last written record of the Franklin expedition. It also contained pills, ointment, medicine and bandages.

Pathfinders

The search for the North Pole

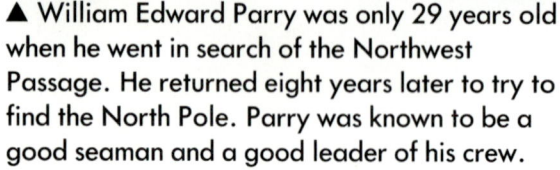

▲ William Edward Parry was only 29 years old when he went in search of the Northwest Passage. He returned eight years later to try to find the North Pole. Parry was known to be a good seaman and a good leader of his crew.

In 1827, Parry returned to the Arctic. The purpose of this journey was to try to reach the North Pole. He had thought of a new way of moving through the ice-covered waters. He built a ship which could either be sailed on the water, or pulled over the ice. It had metal strips on its bottom so that people could pull it over the ice. It was hard work pulling the ship but the crew were helped by the ice itself. The ice was like a moving platform. It drifted towards the Pole four times more quickly than Parry's crew could pull their ship. They pulled the ship for 26 days, but they had 684 km still to go. Parry knew that they could go no further because the crew were too tired, so he turned back.

The moving ice

People began to think about the way the ice moved across the Arctic Ocean. Would it move across the North Pole? Could people reach the Pole by sitting in their ships locked in the ice? Perhaps the ice itself would carry the ships to their goal.

The search for the North Pole

Three years later, an Inuit found pieces of the wreck of the *Jeannette* in faraway Greenland. Pieces must have drifted there over the North Pole from near the New Siberian Islands. De Long's idea had been right.

A boat for the ice

A young man from Norway called Fridtjof Nansen heard about the *Jeannette*. He wanted to try to reach the North Pole by the same method, but he knew he needed a special ship. He built a small and short ship called the *Fram*. It had smooth sides and rounded ends. This was good in ice-covered waters because the ice could not grip the *Fram* and crush it. Nansen did not want the *Fram* to finish its journey like the *Jeannette*.

▲ After the *Jeannette* became locked in the ice, de Long and his men had to march across the ice to Siberia. It was very hard and tiring work to drag the sledges across the uneven, frozen ground. The picture was drawn from a description given by one of the survivors.

In 1879, an American captain named George de Long set out in his ship, the *Jeannette*, to test this idea. He hoped to drift with the ice from the New Siberian Islands to the Pole. He did not get very far. The *Jeannette* was locked in the ice for nearly two years, and then the ice crushed it. De Long had to leave the ship and walk across the ice to Siberia. Only 12 of the crew reached Siberia alive. De Long himself died on the ice.

▲ The *Fram* was designed to withstand the pressure of the crushing ice of the Arctic Ocean. The ship was built to be as small and strong as possible. Nansen wanted the *Fram* to be just big enough to hold coal and food for 12 men for five years.

13

Pathfinders

Nansen and the *Fram*

Nansen started the long drift in the *Fram* in September 1893. He began the journey just north of the New Siberian Islands, like de Long had done.

The *Fram* drifted for months in the ice. The crew got used to the sounds of the cracking ice and the creaking noise of the ship. In the winter, they did not see daylight for many weeks. During the time they were drifting, they printed a newspaper and had parties on their birthdays. They climbed out of the ship on to the ice and hunted polar bears, but there was little to do but wait and drift with the ice.

The *Fram* reached latitude 84° north in April 1895. It had been drifting for almost 18 months. Nansen knew that they were now drifting west, not north. The *Fram* would not drift to the Pole, so Nansen decided to try to walk to the Pole over the ice.

Nansen leaves the *Fram*

Nansen left the *Fram* and took along one of his crew called Hjalmar Johansen. They took three sledges, 27 dogs and two small boats, called **kayaks**, with them.

At first, Nansen and Johansen made good progress over the smooth ice. Then, the ice became uneven and this slowed them down. Their fingers and toes were frozen and they both had **frostbite**. Worst of all, the ice was drifting quickly away from the Pole.

They got to within 363 km of the Pole, but could not get nearer. They had got closer to the Pole than anyone else before them.

The journey back

Nansen knew that he would not find the *Fram* where he had left it. It had drifted away with the ice. He and Johansen headed for Franz Josef Land, 664 km away. They hoped they would find people there to help them.

Nansen and the *Fram*

▲ Nansen had made earlier trips across the Greenland ice pack before he decided to set out for the North Pole. In this group, Nansen is seated in the centre of the picture. In front of him, are skis and snowshoes. Snowshoes are used to stop people from sinking into deep snow.

Both men made a long journey across the ice. They ran short of food, and once they lost their compass. They spent two days going back to find it. When they reached the end of the solid **ice pack**, they used their kayaks. Nansen and Johansen reached a small island, but no one was living there. It was too cold to travel, so they lived on the island through the winter in a stone hut. They were glad to be on solid land again and to be able to hunt seals and polar bears for food.

Nansen and Johansen set off again in their kayaks in May 1896. This time, they found an island with people living there. They were safe at last.

Meanwhile, the *Fram* had broken out of the ice at about the same time as Nansen and Johansen reached safety. The little ship had been caught in the ice for nearly 1000 days. All her crew came home to Norway safely.

▲ A walrus attacking Nansen's kayak. Walruses were a constant danger to Nansen and Johansen because they were very fierce. One walrus did make a hole in Nansen's kayak. He just got out before the kayak sank.

◀ Nansen's cabin on the *Fram* as it now appears in the Fram Museum in Oslo, Norway. His thick wool trousers and jacket helped to protect him from the cold Arctic conditions. The instruments helped him to find his position and keep records of the temperature and the wind speed.

15

Pathfinders

The Northwest Passage at last

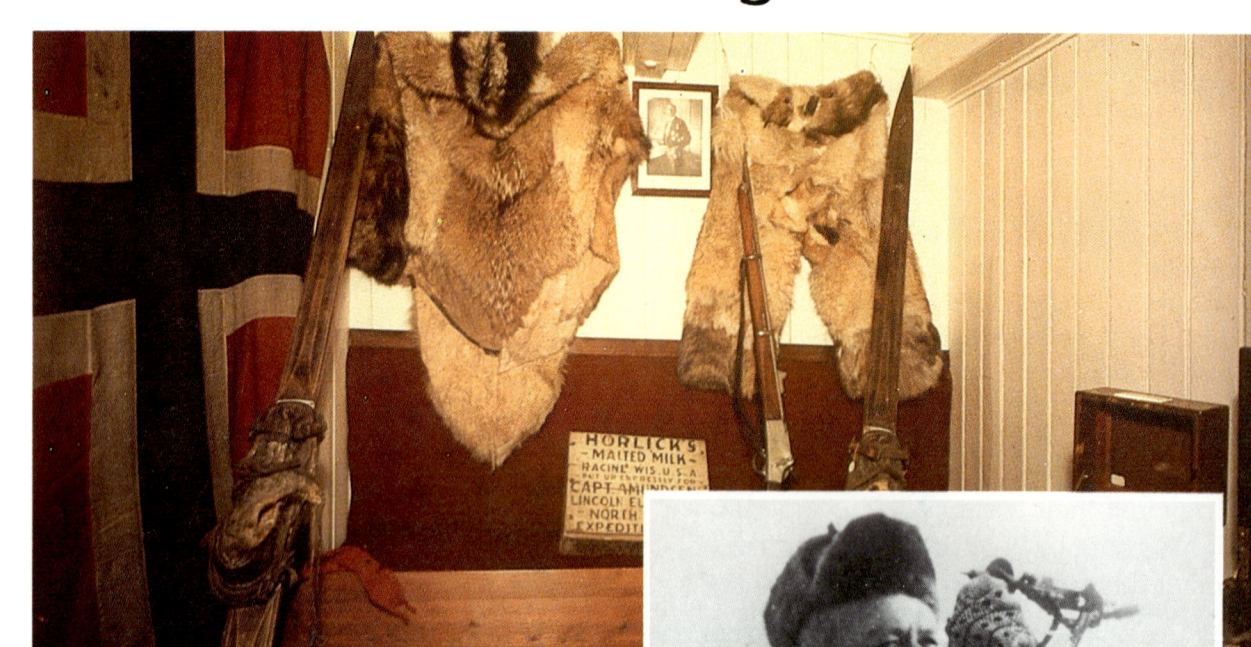

▲ Amundsen's cabin as it now appears in the Fram Museum in Oslo, Norway. His fur polar suit is hanging on the wall. Amundsen learned from the Inuit that animal skins were warm, but light to wear.

A young man in Norway named Roald Amundsen read about the journeys of Franklin and Nansen. He wanted to be the first person to sail through the Northwest Passage, and also to reach the North Pole.

Amundsen was the son of a sea captain and a very good sailor. He also became a good skier, which was a skill he would need on his long journeys over the snow and ice. He did all he could to get ready for the bitter cold of the Arctic. He even slept with his windows open in the winter to get used to the cold. In Norway, the winter nights are very cold.

▲ Amundsen in his polar clothing. He is taking a reading with his sextant. The sextant gave him the angle between the horizon and the Sun or a star. From this angle, he could work out his position.

The Northwest Passage at last

The secret departure

Amundsen planned to sail to the Arctic. He spent a lot of money getting ready and owed money to many people. These people would not let Amundsen leave unless he paid them first. In 1903, he sailed away in secret, but he did pay what he owed them when he came back.

Amundsen's ship was called the *Gjöa*, and it had a small crew of six. They took 17 dogs with them to help pull the sledges over the ice. Amundsen almost lost the *Gjöa* when it ran on to some rocks which were hidden under the sea. To allow the ship to float, Amundsen had to throw some of his supplies into the sea to make the ship lighter. At last, it sailed off the rocks.

Amundsen continued with his journey. He made friends with some Inuit. He learned a lot from them about how to live in the polar regions. They showed him how to dress in caribou skins to keep warm.

The Northwest Passage

Amundsen's main aim was to try to find a way through the Northwest Passage from the Arctic to the Pacific Ocean. To do this, they had to find a way through the pack ice along the coast of North Canada. In places, the water was very shallow, so Amundsen sent a small boat ahead of the *Gjöa*. A sailor in the boat let a rope down into the water with a lead weight on the end. With this, they could tell how deep the water was. Once, there was only 2½ cm of water under the bottom of the *Gjöa*.

At last, Amundsen saw the masts of an American ship ahead of them. This ship had come from the Pacific, so Amundsen knew he had succeeded. He was the first person to sail through the Northwest Passage.

Amundsen wanted to tell the people of Norway what he had done. He had to go by sledge for about 1000 km across Alaska to send a message. When Amundsen came back to the *Gjöa*, he sailed on down the west coast of Canada and the United States to San Francisco. He gave the *Gjöa* to the people there. It would remind them that it was Amundsen who had found the Northwest Passage.

◀ Amundsen is boiling water on a stove next to his tent during the expedition. His skis and sledge are behind him. The Norwegian flag is on his tent.

Pathfinders
The US and the North Pole

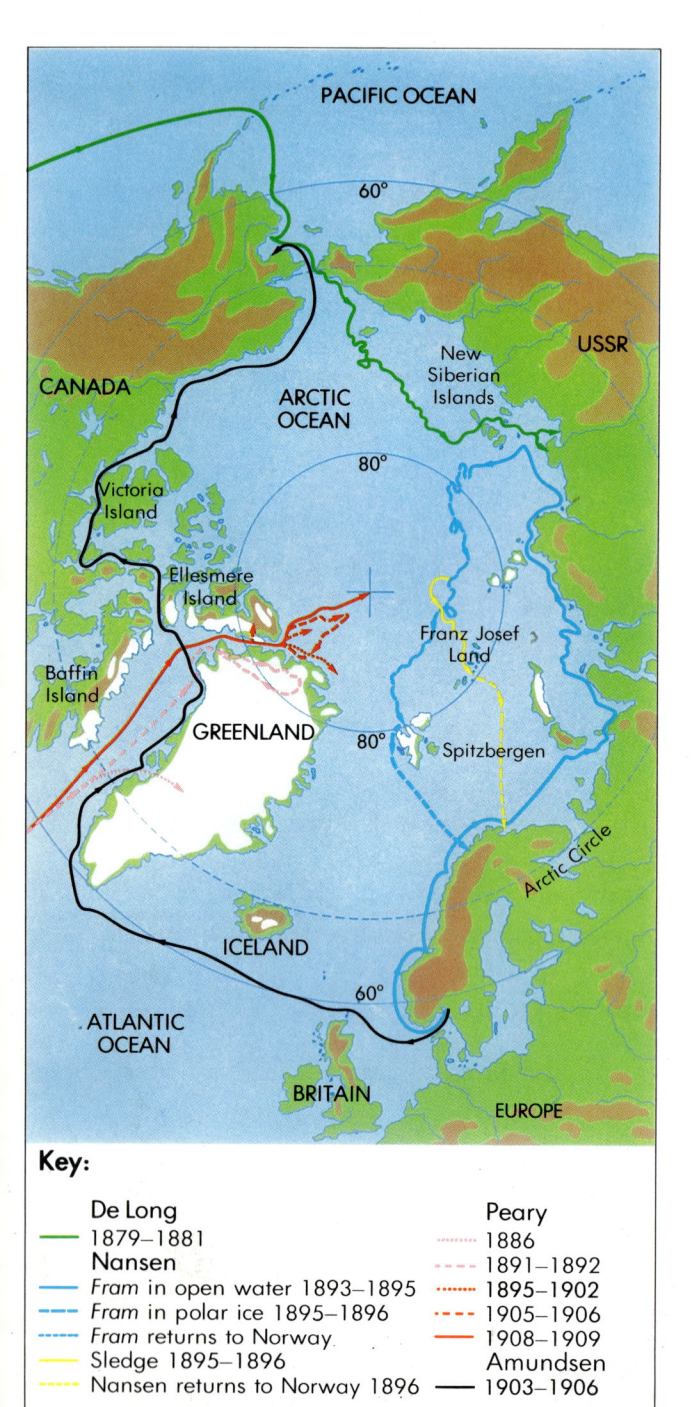

Map key:

Key:
De Long
— 1879–1881
Nansen
— Fram in open water 1893–1895
-- Fram in polar ice 1895–1896
···· Fram returns to Norway
— Sledge 1895–1896
---- Nansen returns to Norway 1896

Peary
···· 1886
---- 1891–1892
···· 1895–1902
— 1905–1906
— 1908–1909
Amundsen
— 1903–1906

Explorers from many countries hoped for a chance to reach the North Pole. One of these was Robert Peary from the United States. Peary always wanted to explore. As a young man, he had joined the US Navy. He hoped the navy would teach him some of the skills an explorer must have.

Peary made many trips to Greenland. His first visit was in 1886. He learned a lot about living in snow and ice from the Inuit there. Peary understood that these people knew more than anyone else about how to survive in the Arctic. Later, he wore Inuit clothes and ate Inuit food.

In 1891, he went back again to Greenland with his wife, Jo. They lived with the Inuit, and their first baby was born there. On this visit, Peary made a journey to the north of Greenland. Some people thought that Greenland stretched all the way to the North Pole. Peary proved that Greenland was an island, and that it did not stretch to the Pole.

◀ The routes of the explorers who tried to reach the North Pole. Robert Peary was the first to reach the North Pole on 6 April 1909.

▶ In the Arctic, Peary's crew had to hunt for their food. In the past, the Inuit people used to hunt the walrus because it provided them with many essential items. They got ivory and bone for their tools, leather for their ropes and kayak covers, and skins for their clothes. They also got oil for their lamps and stoves and a good supply of meat.

The US and the North Pole

Frostbite

In 1898, Peary was sailing inside the Arctic Circle on his ship, the *Windward*. The ship was stopped by ice, so Peary chose to go on by sledge to the US **base** on Ellesmere Island. It was winter, and he travelled in the moonlight. It was very cold, and Peary had severe frostbite. When he reached the US base, he was in great pain. There was a doctor at the base, named Frederick Cook. He was also a polar explorer. Dr Cook took care of Peary, but he had to cut off eight of Peary's toes because of the frostbite.

Peary feared he would never walk again, but he wrote, 'I shall find a way, or make one'. He would not give up. In 1902, he tried to reach the North Pole using sledges from Ellesmere Island. He came within 288 km of his goal. He had broken all the records so far.

A new ship

In 1905, President Theodore Roosevelt of the United States asked Peary to try again to reach the North Pole. Peary set out with a new ship called the *Roosevelt*. It was built to smash through ice. As well as his crew, Peary invited some Inuit and took some **husky dogs** from Siberia with him. These dogs are used to living in the snow and ice.

When the pack ice became thick, Peary left the *Roosevelt* and started off across the ice to the Pole. He was unlucky. The weather became very bad, and Peary and his men could travel only eight kilometres a day. He reached latitude 87° north, but he had to turn back. He knew he would not have enough food.

▼ Commander Robert Peary on board his ship, the *Roosevelt*. The ship was built for his 1905 expedition.

Pathfinders

First at the North Pole?

Peary did not give up trying to reach the North Pole. He still wanted to reach there before anyone else. He set off in the *Roosevelt* again in 1908. The journey was very well planned. When he reached the ice pack, he sent parties of men ahead of him towards the Pole to leave supplies of food along the route. These were called **advance parties**.

The advance parties had finished their work in March 1909, and Peary set off. He took with him 26 men, 28 sledges and 140 dogs to help pull the sledges. Supplies of food and fuel were loaded on to these sledges. Peary did not intend to take all the men with him to the Pole.

Most of them were **support groups**. Their job was to help Peary to bring supplies as near to the Pole as possible. Peary would need these supplies for the journey back.

Peary and his party had a hard journey. At one point, the sea had broken through, and made a gap in the ice. Peary and his men cut out large pieces of ice and made them into ice rafts. They floated on these across the gap to the next stretch of ice.

At latitude 88° north, Peary sent the last support party back to the *Roosevelt*. He went on to the North Pole with four Inuit and another American called Matthew Henson.

▼ Peary and his men with their dog teams at the beginning of their march across the bumpy ice ridges.

First at the North Pole?

Who won?

Peary and his party had 195 km to cover before they reached the Pole. They made good progress, and at last on 6 April 1909, they stood at the North Pole. Peary wrote in his diary, 'The Pole at last. My dream and goal for 20 years. Mine at last'. Peary and his party stayed at the Pole for 30 hours. Then, they set off for the *Roosevelt*.

When Peary got home to the United States, he heard that Dr Cook claimed to have reached the Pole a year before him. Peary knew Dr Cook. He was the doctor who had saved his life by removing eight of his toes 11 years before. There was a big argument, but most people think that Peary was really the first person to reach the North Pole.

A change of plan

In Norway, Amundsen had planned a journey to the North Pole. He was going to sail in the *Fram*, which was Nansen's old ship. He changed his plans when he heard about Peary's success. Amundsen liked keeping secrets. He puzzled his crew when he told them to prepare for hot weather. Later, he told them the reason. They were going to cross the Equator and head for the South Pole instead of the North Pole. The crew were very pleased when they heard Amundsen's new plan.

▲ Peary's men at the North Pole. From left to right, Ooqueak, Ootah, Matthew Henson, Egingwah, Seegloo. Henson is carrying the American flag, which Peary's wife had made for the expedition. Peary buried a strip of the flag at the North Pole.

◀ The front page of the *New York Times*, from 7 September 1909, with the report that Peary had reached the North Pole. News of Peary's success reached the United States five months after the event.

21

Pathfinders

Antarctica

If you go as far south in the world as possible, you will come to a great mass of land, or **continent**, called Antarctica. The South Pole is near the middle of this huge, frozen land. The land is covered with a great sheet of ice. This ice is very thick. In many places, you would have to dig a hole through the ice about 1.6 km deep to find the soil and rock. If all that ice melted and became water, the oceans of the world would rise at least 45 m. A lot of low-lying land would be covered by the sea.

Antarctica lies inside the Antarctic Circle. It is at the bottom of the world, 960 km from the nearest land. It has the coldest and windiest climate in the world. From March to October, it is winter and there is hardly any daylight.

In the Arctic Circle, there are towns and cities, but there are none inside the Antarctic Circle. The only people you will find there are scientists carrying out **experiments**.

▼ Fur seals in South Georgia, Antarctica. Fur seals are quiet creatures. They can swim for long distances, and are good at finding their way.

Antarctica

Stories of a southern continent

For hundreds of years, people thought there might be a great land in the south. About 1300 years ago, people from the islands in the South Pacific Ocean went on long voyages in big canoes to try to find this land. They brought back stories of a 'foggy, misty and dark place not shone on by the Sun'. Maori people in New Zealand told stories of a great white land to the south. We do not know if any of these people reached Antarctica itself. It does not seem likely that they could have got there through the ice-covered seas in their open boats.

South of the Antarctic Circle

In January 1773, a British sailor called Captain James Cook went south of the Antarctic Circle. He was sailing in his ship, the *Resolution*. Cook wrote about stormy seas and huge areas of pack ice and icebergs. He also said that there were many seals living there. Cook sailed all around Antarctica, but he never saw the continent. It was too risky to try to sail further south in his small wooden boat. Cook did not think that there could be any land worth finging in such a cold and gloomy place.

▲ A photograph of the Antarctic taken on the Transglobe Expedition. It shows one of the many crevasses in the ice which are a great danger to explorers.

▲ Captain James Cook was a very good seaman. In 1774, he went on a second voyage to the South Pacific Ocean in search of a southern continent.

Pathfinders

The first sight of Antarctica

Cook's reports had said that there were many seals in the cold seas in the south. Many people wanted to hunt seals for their skins. The skins were worth a lot of money in Europe and the United States. Seal hunters went to the Antarctic seas. In their search for seals, they found many islands which no one had seen before. The early seal hunters did not reach the huge land of Antarctica, but one of them, William Smith, came very close. In 1819, he found the South Shetland Islands, which are not far from the coast of Antarctica.

Voyages for science

Scientists in Europe and the United States wanted to find out more about the area inside the Antarctic Circle. In 1838, six ships sailed towards the Antarctic from the United States. Their leader was Charles Wilkes. Wilkes was not very well prepared for the journey ahead. He did not have ships which could sail well in icy and stormy seas. One ship hit an iceberg and sank. Other ships became top-heavy because too much ice formed on their masts and ropes. None of the ships had enough room under the decks for people to live and sleep in the cold weather. Wilkes did not bring enough warm clothes for his crew, and the food ran short. By the time he reached the Antarctic Circle, he had only three ships left.

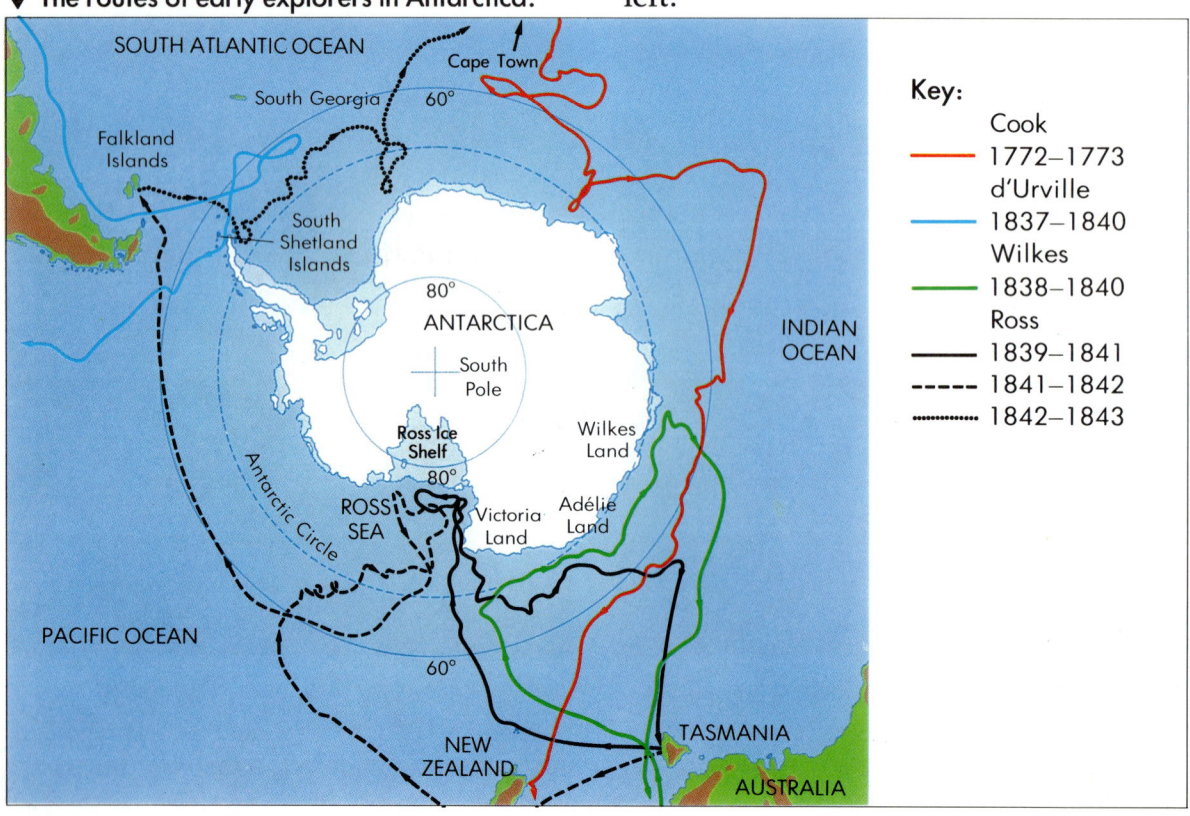

▼ The routes of early explorers in Antarctica.

The first sight of Antarctica

◀ Charles Wilkes was commander of the United States expedition to the Antarctic in 1838. Wilkes sailed with three warships, two smaller ships and a supply ship. The ships were built for warmer seas, and were not suitable for the stormy Antarctic waters.

New finds

Much had gone wrong on Wilkes' voyage, but he had one great success. He was the first man to see the mainland of Antarctica on 19 January 1840. He called the part of the coast which he saw 'Adélie Land' after his wife Adélie.

When Wilkes got back to the United States, he heard that a Frenchman, called Jules d'Urville, had seen Antarctica on 18 January, one day before Wilkes. Later, people found out that d'Urville had made a mistake about his dates. He had seen Antarctica on 19 January, a few hours after Wilkes.

A British explorer, James Ross, also led a voyage to Antarctica, which lasted for four years, from 1839 to 1843. Ross found the Ross **Ice Shelf**. This is a sheet of ice about 150 m thick which stretches from the land and covers the sea. The ice shelf is twice as big as New Zealand. Later, people set off from the Ross Ice Shelf to explore Antarctica.

◀ Jules d'Urville had planned to take two corvettes, the *Astrolabe* and the *Zelée*, to explore the warm seas of the South Pacific. Then, King Louis-Philippe of France ordered that d'Urville should explore the Antarctic region. The ships were away for three years and d'Urville claimed Adélie Land for France.

Pathfinders

The two rivals

After Ross came back to Britain in 1843, few people sailed south to Antarctica for over 50 years. Then, in 1901, there was a new expedition to Antarctica. It was led by Robert Scott, and Ernest Shackleton was one of his party. After this expedition, the two men split up, and Shackleton led expeditions of his own.

▲ Captain Robert Scott was born in England in 1868. He was not a strong man, but he drove himself harder than any of his men.

Captain Scott

Captain Robert Scott was an officer in the British Royal Navy. He wanted to achieve something important and become famous. When Scott was 31, he met a man called Markham, who was planning to send an expedition to the Antarctic. Markham asked Scott to lead the expedition.

For the next year, Scott read as much as he could about Antarctica and spoke to many people who had been to the polar regions. A ship named the *Discovery* was built for the journey. In 1901, Scott set off in the *Discovery* with Ernest Shackleton among his crew.

The two rivals

Scott's journey was a success in many ways. He made maps of 1900 km of coastline. He and his party also pulled sledges across the Ross Ice Shelf and up on to the frozen level ground, or **plateau**, of Antarctica. He reached latitude 82° south, 320 km further south than anyone else before him. Scott even brought a hot air balloon with him. In this, he floated up to 245 m above the ice. From that height, he could see further across the icy plateau of Antarctica.

Ernest Shackleton

While Scott and Shackleton were on the Ross Ice Shelf, they had a quarrel. Shackleton was suffering from a disease called **scurvy**. People can get scurvy if they do not eat the right kind of vegetables and fresh fruit, especially oranges and lemons. Shackleton thought it was Scott's fault that he had scurvy because Scott had not brought enough fresh fruit with him. Scott sent Shackleton back to the *Discovery* so that he would get better. Shackleton was upset, and thought he would be a better leader than Scott. From then on, the two men were rivals.

▼ The hot air balloon that Scott took with him to the Antarctic. This was the first balloon ever to take off from an ice field.

▲ The Ross Ice Shelf in Antarctica is like a cliff of ice which rises about 50 to 70 m above the level of the sea. The shelf is moving all the time, and large pieces are broken off it by the tide. The Ross Ice Shelf was named after James Ross. He first saw the Ice Shelf on his voyage to Antarctica in 1841.

Pathfinders

Shackleton alone

Scott and Shackleton went home to Britain in 1904. Right away, Shackleton began planning his own expedition. Shackleton was an Irishman, who loved being with people. His men called him 'the Boss'. They loved and trusted him.

In 1907, Shackleton and his crew sailed for the Antarctic in the *Nimrod*, a small ship weighing 200 tonnes. He brought some ponies with him and a motor car! The car soon proved to be useless in the snow and ice.

▼ Shackleton and his men take a rest while they set up camp. Shackleton planned his expedition to the Antarctic very well. He took the right food supplies so his men would not get ill.

When the men reached Antarctica, they divided into three groups. One group set out to climb Mount Erebus, which is 3794 m high. From the top of this mountain, they would get a better view of the land around them. It took six days to reach the top. The men got down again in only one day by sliding down the snow and ice.

The South Magnetic Pole

Another group of Shackleton's men wanted to reach the South Magnetic Pole. When you look at a compass to see which direction is south, you are really looking at the direction of the South Magnetic Pole. The true south of the world is the South Pole, which is not the same place as the South Magnetic Pole.

Shackleton's men had to climb up sheets of ice, called **glaciers**, which spread down the mountain sides. The men were worn out, but they trusted 'the Boss' and kept going. At last, on 16 January 1909, they reached the South Magnetic Pole.

▼ The routes of Ernest Shackleton, Robert Scott and Roald Amundsen in their journeys to the South Pole. The first person to reach the South Pole was Roald Amundsen on 14 December 1911.

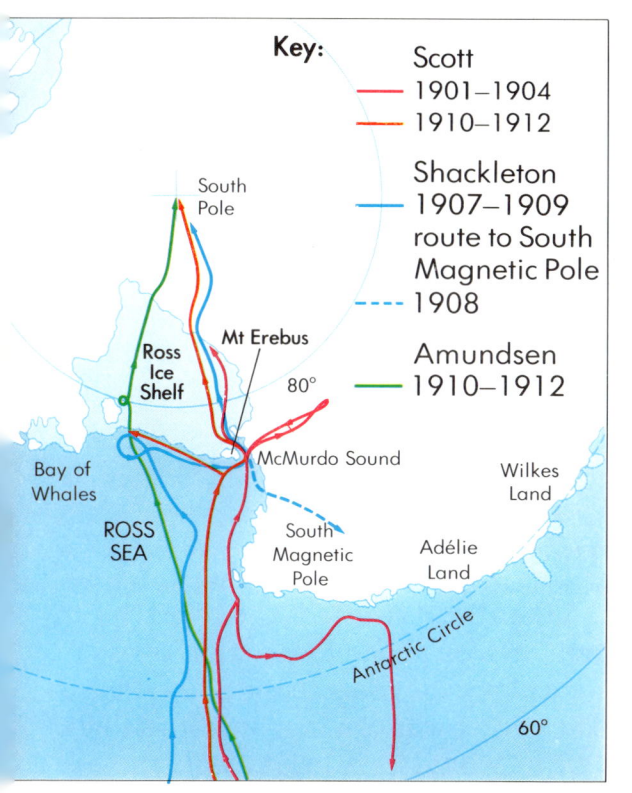

Shackleton turns back

Shackleton planned another journey, this time to the South Pole itself. He set off with three other men and some ponies to pull their sledges. At first, they made good progress. The sun was shining as they crossed the Ross Ice Shelf. It was so warm that they could even take off their coats! Then, they had to climb up on to the plateau. They found a new route up a glacier which they called the Beardmore Glacier. It was a dangerous journey. Sometimes, there were splits in the ice which were more than a kilometre deep. These splits are called **crevasses**. Often, the crevasses were covered over by thin ice. One of Shackleton's ponies fell down a crevasse. It was lucky that the sledge the pony was pulling did not fall down, too. This sledge was carrying all the food.

Shackleton reached the plateau on Christmas Day 1908. He was only 160 km from the South Pole, but he had to turn back. He did not want to risk his men's lives. If they went on, they would not have enough food for the journey back to the ship.

Shackleton and his men reached the *Nimrod* after a return journey of 1120 km. They were 117 days late. The captain of the *Nimrod* had worried that they were all dead.

◀ A sketch made of Shackleton's expedition at their camp. In the background are some of the Siberian ponies which were taken along by Shackleton to carry the supplies.

Pathfinders

The race to the South Pole

In 1909, people in Britain heard the news of Shackleton's successes in the Antarctic. Then, there came the news that Peary had reached the North Pole. These two pieces of news made Scott decide to go to Antarctica again to try to be the first person to reach the South Pole.

People in Britain gave Scott money for a new journey to the South Pole. Ten thousand people wanted to join Scott, but he could only take less than 100. He set off in June 1910 in a ship called the *Terra Nova*. Scott carried motor sledges on board as well as dogs, because he thought that it would be cruel to force dogs to pull sledges all the way to the South Pole. He was unlucky because he lost 292 gallons of fuel for the sledges in a storm at sea only three days after leaving Britain.

On the way to Antarctica, Scott received a message from Amundsen. Amundsen was turning south in the *Fram* to head for the South Pole. Amundsen had changed his plans to reach the North Pole after he heard that Peary had already reached it. Now, the journey to the South Pole had become a race.

The emperor penguins

When Scott reached Antarctica, he sent men on ahead to leave supplies of food along the route to the South Pole. The winter was coming, and Scott knew that he would have to wait until the spring before heading for the Pole.

▲ Scott's ship, the *Terra Nova* at McMurdo Sound.

▶ These sketches of emperor penguins were made by Edward Wilson on Scott's last expedition to the South Pole. The emperor penguin is the largest of the many types of penguin found in Antarctica.

The race to the South Pole

It is winter in Antarctica in May, June and July. It is very cold and dark during these months. Even so, Scott wanted to use the time to find out more about Antarctica. On 27 June, in the middle of the winter, three men set off by sledge across the frozen sea. The men were 'Birdie' Bowers, Edward Wilson and Apsley Cherry-Garrard. They travelled for nearly 100 km to a place where the emperor penguins built their nests. The temperature of −60 °C was very cold. The men's clothes became frozen stiff. They built a small wooden hut, but a storm blew the roof off. They had to lie in sleeping bags for two days, and wait for the storm to end. When the storm was over, they were able to get back to Scott safely.

Seven months in an ice cave

Six of Scott's men went to study rocks on another part of the coast of Antarctica. They expected to stay there for six weeks. When the *Terra Nova* tried to pick them up again, the ship could not get to them through the frozen sea. The six men dug a tunnel into the ice and made a cave. They lived in this through the winter. They had to kill seals and penguins for food. When the spring came, all six men were able to get back to join Scott.

Scott and his party had to wait until November 1911 for the winter to end before they could set off for the South Pole again.

▲ A charcoal sketch by Edward Wilson, one of the men on Scott's expedition. It shows three men cramped together in one tent to keep warm.

Pathfinders

Amundsen arrives

Amundsen sailed south in the *Fram* and reached a place called the Bay of Whales in January 1911. This was nearly 100 km nearer to the Pole than Scott had been. Amundsen had brought 97 husky dogs with him. These dogs were to pull the sledges across the ice. Amundsen had also chosen his men with great care. Unlike Scott's men, they were all good skiers. Amundsen had planned the expedition much better than Scott had.

Amundsen sent people ahead to leave food supplies on the route to the Pole before the winter set in. His men walked and the dogs pulled the sledges. When they had dropped the supplies, the men sat on the sledges and the dogs pulled them back to Amundsen's base camp.

The long wait

When the winter set in, Amundsen and his men waited in the huts they had built at their base camp in the Bay of Whales. He did not send his men out on long journeys in the middle of the winter, as Scott had done. He wanted to build up their strength. He made sure his men ate good food with plenty of vegetables and fruit to avoid scurvy.

In August, the sun rose again over the horizon after the long, dark winter was over. Amundsen wanted to leave in September. It was still very cold, −56 °C, so he waited for another month.

▼ It is important to keep warm on polar expeditions. At night, Scott's men slept in fur sleeping bags. Here, Evans on the left and Crean on the right, are mending their sleeping bags back at the base camp.

Amundsen arrives

Scott sets off

On 1 November 1911, Scott had started at last for the South Pole. Things went wrong almost at once. The motor sledges broke down in the bitter cold. Then, a snowstorm with strong winds, called a **blizzard**, stopped them for five days. Scott and his men had to use up some of their precious food supplies while they waited for the blizzard to end. When Scott reached the Beardmore Glacier, he sent the dogs back to the base camp with some of his men. He continued up the glacier with three groups of four men. Each group pulled a sledge weighing about 400 kg. Sometimes, it took them hours to cover a few hundred metres because the glacier was so steep.

When Scott was 320 km from the Pole, he sent back the last support party. He went on with four men, even though he was short of food.

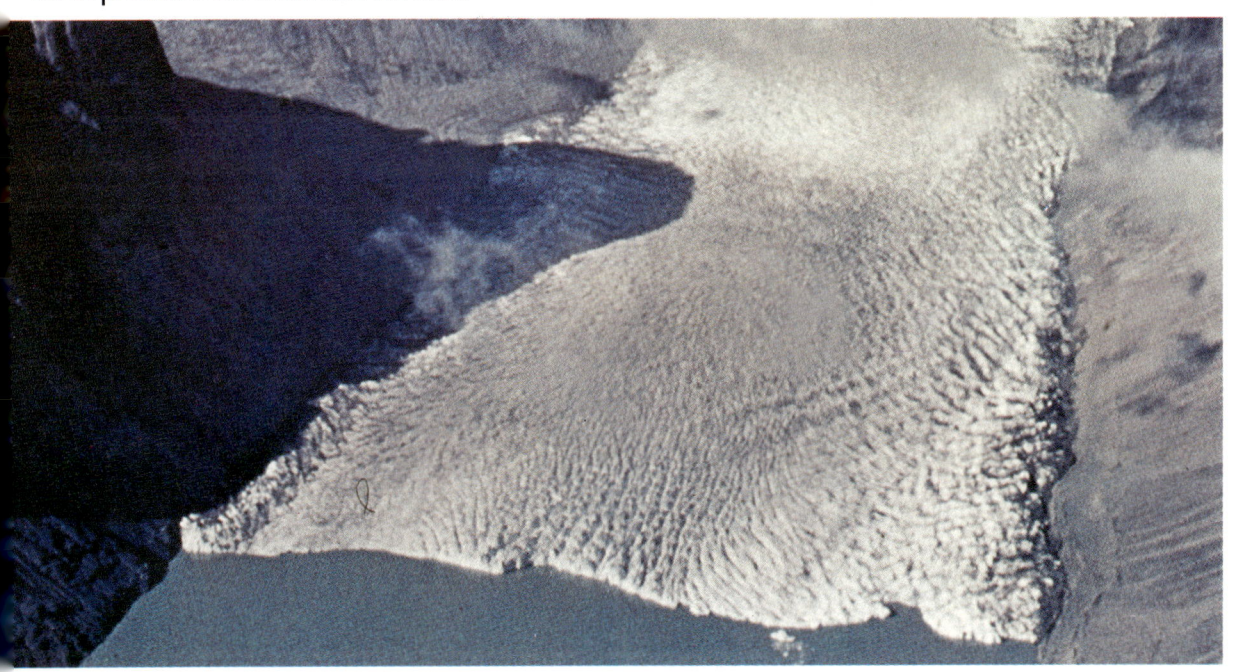

▲ Two of Scott's men are trying to start one of their motor sledges. These sledges often broke down in the bitter cold.

▼ Glaciers like this one in Antarctica caused a lot of problems for Scott and his men.

Pathfinders

Struggle and success

Amundsen set off for the South Pole on 19 October 1911, 13 days before Scott. He had only four men with him from the start of the journey. He took 52 husky dogs to pull his sledges which were loaded with supplies of food.

Amundsen soon met trouble on his journey. He almost lost a sledge down a crevasse on the Ross Ice Shelf. One of his party fell into a crevasse. The man was lucky that he did not fall to the bottom. He saved himself by holding on to one of the sides.

When Amundsen and his men had crossed the Ross Ice Shelf, they had to make the long climb up to the plateau. This climb took them four days.

▼ Roald Amundsen in his polar clothing on his way to the South Pole in 1911.

The use of husky dogs

Amundsen relied on dogs to pull his sledges. He had started for the Pole with 52 dogs, but he planned to return with only 12. He could not bring enough food with him for all the dogs on such a long journey, so he had to shoot the dogs when he had no food left for them.

Some people think that it was cruel to shoot the dogs. Captain Scott thought so, and he took fewer dogs with him when he set off for the Pole. When he had no food left for the dogs, he sent them back to base camp with some of his men. This was kind to the dogs, but it was hard on his party. Scott and his men pulled the sledges themselves. This made the journey much slower and more tiring for Scott's party than for Amundsen and his men.

Struggle and success

The South Pole conquered

When Amundsen and his men reached the plateau, they made good progress. They became excited as they passed the furthest point reached by Shackleton in 1908. Once, they thought they could see Scott ahead, but it was only their eyes playing tricks on them. At last, on 14 December 1911, the party reached latitude 90° south, the South Pole. Amundsen proudly put the flag of Norway in the snow. The men spent two days exploring the area, and then hurried back to give the news to the world.

▼ Roald Amundsen checking his position at the South Pole on 14 December 1911. The Norwegian flag flies in the wind beside him.

Scott did not know of Amundsen's success and continued his journey to the Pole. Scott and his four men had only food for four, and four sets of skis. Their tent was too small for five. Pulling the sledges was very tiring, and they were all half-frozen with cold.

A few kilometres from the Pole, they saw the tracks of Amundsen's dogs in the snow. Scott knew then that he had lost the race. He reached the South Pole on 17 January 1912.

▼ Scott's men at the South Pole with the British flag behind them. The men are sad and tired. After their struggle to get there, they found they were second in the race. From left to right are Lawrence Oates, Henry Bowers, Robert Scott, Edward Wilson and Edgar Evans.

Pathfinders

Scott's last journey

Scott and his men were tired, cold and short of food. Now, they had to face a journey of 1280 km back to their base camp. Scott wrote in his diary, 'I wonder if we can do it'.

The journey became a hard struggle. Pulling the sledges made Scott and his men very weak. The food Scott had brought was not good enough for men doing hard work in extreme cold. The men became weaker and weaker.

One of the men, named Edgar Evans, suffered badly from frostbite. He fell down twice and hurt his head badly. He was a bigger man than the others, and he needed more food to keep up his strength. However, he had only the same amount of food as the other men. Evans soon became so weak that he could not pull the sledge any further. He tried to walk along beside the sledge. He soon became too weak and he fell down. He died in the snow.

The death of Oates

There were now only four men to pull the sledges. As they grew weaker, they made less progress each day. This meant that in order to make their food last, they had to eat even less. As a result, they became even weaker.

When they reached the Ross Ice Shelf, they were all very cold, very weak and

▲ Captain Oates walking out into the blizzard. He died so his three friends, Robert Scott, Edward Wilson and Henry Bowers might live.

very tired. As the winter was coming on, the weather turned colder than before. It was −34 °C even during the day.

Another man in Scott's party named Lawrence Oates was now so weak that he could not pull a sledge. For four days, he walked along beside the sledges, but he was afraid he was holding the others up and risking their lives. One night, he asked them to leave him behind in his sleeping bag. They refused, but then he got up and said, 'I am just going outside, and I may be some time'. They never saw him again. Scott said, 'It was the act of a brave man'.

Scott's last journey

▲ This is the last page from Scott's diary. It was found by his body eight months later by a search party. It says, 'We shall stick it out to the end but we are getting weaker of course, and the end cannot be far. It seems a pity but I do not think I can write more — R. Scott'. The last entry reads, 'For God's sake look after our people'.

A tragic ending

The last three men, Scott, Wilson and Bowers moved on slowly over the ice. On 21 March 1912, they were only 17 km from a food store which would have saved their lives. Then, a blizzard started which lasted nine days. It was impossible to move, and all three men died in their tent.

Eight months later, a search party found them. The three men looked as if they were sleeping. They also found Scott's diary. In it, he said that it was bad luck and not bad planning which had led to the tragedy. The search party built a pile of stones over the three dead men. Their grave is still there on the Ross Ice Shelf.

▲ These are some of Scott's belongings found by the search party. His skis have his initials RFS on them.

Pathfinders

More challenges in the Antarctic

The main goal in Antarctica, the South Pole, had now been reached. What new journeys could explorers make in the Antarctic?

In 1914, Shackleton sailed south in the *Endurance*. He aimed to cross Antarctica from one side to the other. He planned to start his journey at the Weddell Sea.

Shackleton found thick pack ice in the Weddell Sea, and the *Endurance* became stuck in the ice about 100 km from land. Shackleton knew that they were in great danger as millions of tonnes of ice pushed against the ship. He was a good leader. He kept his 28 men busy and happy with hunting trips and concerts. They even played games of football on the ice.

The end of the *Endurance*

The *Endurance* drifted in the ice for 281 days and moved 1000 km. In the end, it was crushed when it was about 500 km from the nearest land. Shackleton and his crew left the ship with three lifeboats, which they pulled across the drifting ice. They could only move about three

◀ Shackleton's ship, the *Endurance*, was built specially for the 1914 expedition. Shackleton and his men stayed on board the ship through the winter when they were caught in pack ice. Finally, the ice crushed the ship. Shackleton's crew had to take all their sledges, boats and supplies off the ship.

More challenges in the Antarctic

kilometres a day, so they decided to stop and make a camp on the ice. Shackleton called it Ocean Camp. They stayed at Ocean Camp for two months, but then the ice began to break up. On Christmas Day, they **launched** their boats, but it was still too risky to sail through the pack ice. They had to camp again on the ice for another four months.

At last, there was enough clear water for Shackleton to try again. He launched the boats, and after six days and nights, they reached Elephant Island. They were on dry land, but no one lived on the island.

Rescue

The crew were all weak and hungry, and Shackleton had to get help. With five men, he sailed north to try to find people to help them. For 16 days and 1300 km, Shackleton fought against huge waves and the freezing cold in an open boat. They reached land at last on the island of South Georgia. The men landed on the south side of the island where nobody lived. They had to walk across the mountains to the north side. At last, they reached a **whaling station** and people who could help.

Shackleton rescued his crew on Elephant Island when they had only two days' food left. One of them said later that Shackleton, 'was the greatest leader that ever came on God's earth'. Not one of the crew was lost.

▼ The route Shackleton and his men took to Elephant Island. Shackleton then went on to South Georgia to get help.

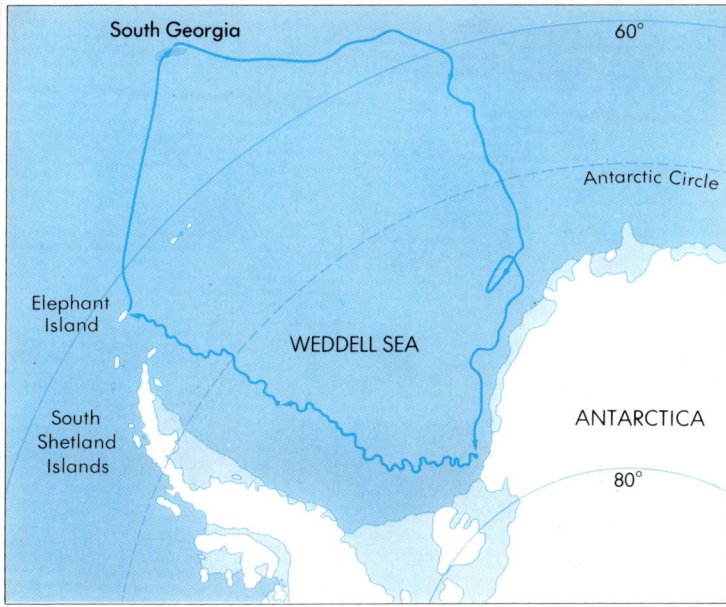

▲ Members of Shackleton's crew after they landed on Elephant Island. Here, they had their first food and drink for three days.

Pathfinders

Flying in polar regions

It was difficult to explore and map the polar regions when people could only move on foot. The **invention** of planes helped people to cover greater distances much more quickly. Also, from high up in the sky, explorers could see much further than they could on the ground. Scott had this in mind when he went up in a hot air balloon in 1902 to a height of 245 m.

The early planes were not as safe as planes are today. It was risky to fly in such cold places as the Arctic or the Antarctic. If planes crashed, it was very hard to reach the pilots and rescue them.

Famous polar fliers

In 1926, the Americans Richard Byrd and Floyd Bennett became the first people to fly in a plane over the North Pole. Later in the same year, an Italian named Umberto Nobile flew over the North Pole in a huge airship called the *Norge*. On board was an American named Lincoln Ellsworth and Roald Amundsen. This famous explorer from Norway had now seen the North Pole as well as the South Pole.

In 1928, Nobile set off again for the North Pole in another airship called the *Italia*. Sadly, he crashed on the way back.

Flying in polar regions

Over the South Pole

Richard Byrd went south to Antarctica and helped to set up an American base on the Ross Ice Shelf between 1928 and 1929. The US team called their camp 'Little America'.

In November 1929, Richard Byrd and two others set off from Little America to try to fly over the South Pole. Byrd called this plane the *Floyd Bennett*, after the pilot who had flown with him over the North Pole. As the plane slowly flew upwards from the Ross Ice Shelf, Byrd feared that it would not climb high enough to rise above the plateau. He threw a week's supply of food out of the plane to make it lighter. The plane climbed higher at once, and then flew up over the plateau. When Byrd reached the Pole, he dropped an American and a British flag, in honour of Scott and his party. The journey around the Pole took ten hours. Byrd said later that there is nothing interesting to see at the South Pole. He wrote, 'It is the effort to get there that counts'.

Since Byrd's first flight in Antarctica, planes have been used a lot to study the area and make maps.

▲ Richard Byrd beside his stove in Little America.

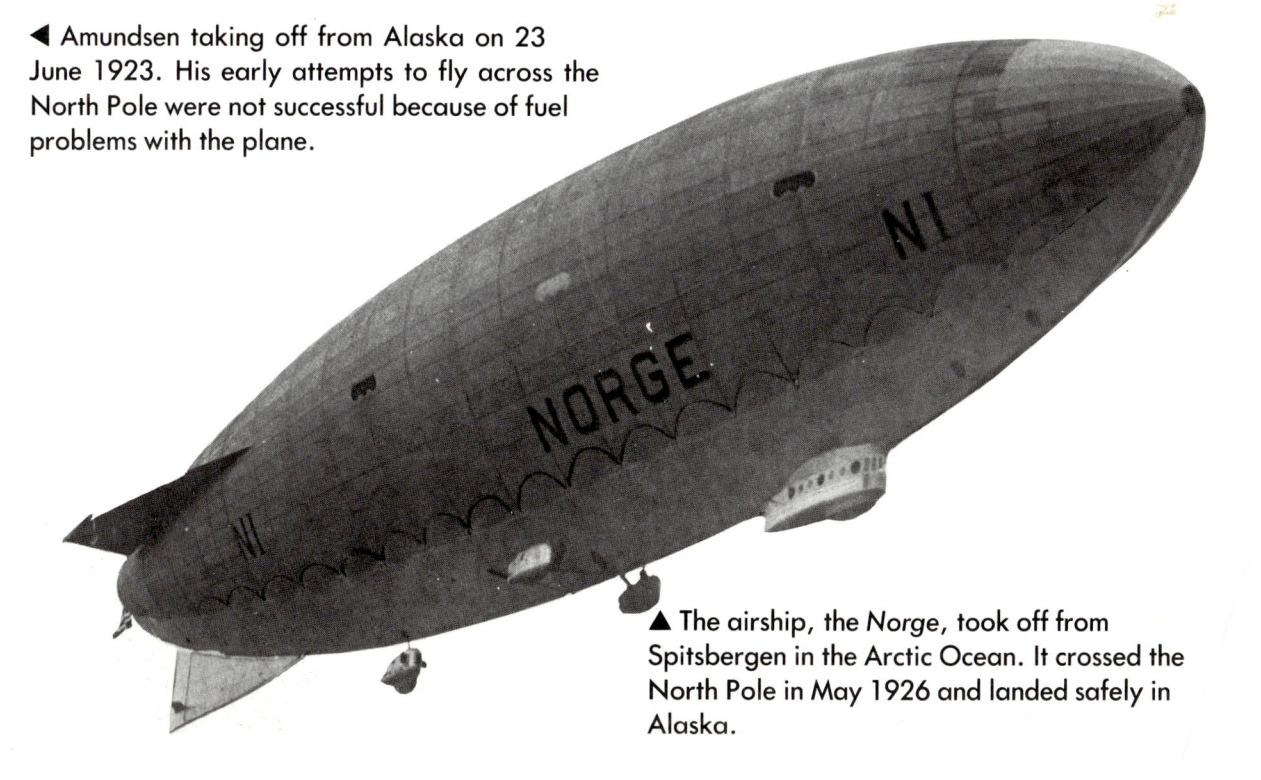

◀ Amundsen taking off from Alaska on 23 June 1923. His early attempts to fly across the North Pole were not successful because of fuel problems with the plane.

▲ The airship, the *Norge*, took off from Spitsbergen in the Arctic Ocean. It crossed the North Pole in May 1926 and landed safely in Alaska.

Pathfinders

New challenges

The early explorers like Nansen, Peary, Shackleton, Scott and Amundsen wanted to be first to reach the Poles. Later, explorers wanted to find out more about the region and to make maps of areas that no one had visited before. In 1946, Richard Byrd led a big party of 4700 men and 13 ships to Antarctica. With the help of planes, he studied 22 400 km of the Antarctic coast. Byrd found **mountain ranges** and islands which no one had seen before. The early explorers could not have dreamed of leading such a big and expensive expedition.

Across Antarctica

Shackleton had planned to cross Antarctica in 1914, but he had failed. In 1957, there was a plan to try again. The leader was Dr Vivian Fuchs. In his party was Edmund Hillary, one of the men who climbed Mount Everest, the highest mountain in the world, in 1953. Fuchs wanted to follow Shackleton's planned route starting from the Weddell Sea and going to the South Pole, and then moving on to the Ross Sea. Hillary was to go to the Pole from the other side of Antarctica. His flight to the Pole began from the Ross Sea.

Fuchs set off with Sno-Cats, which are very big motor tractors built to travel on snow and ice. They have caterpillar tracks like tanks instead of wheels to stop them from sinking in the snow. Even so, Fuchs made slow progress.

Hillary set off for the Pole from the Ross Sea to meet Fuchs. Fuchs arrived at the Pole and met Hillary there. Fuchs had made a journey of 1500 km from the Weddell Sea. Hillary then flew home, and Fuchs set off on his own for the Ross Sea. He arrived there on 2 March 1958. Fuchs had covered about 3500 km in 99 days.

In 1979, two British adventurers set off to travel around the world from north to south and cross the two Poles. They were Ranulph Fiennes and Charles Burton. They crossed Antarctica by using small open-topped motor sledges called **snowmobiles**. On their journey, Burton's snowmobile fell down a crevasse and was lost. Fiennes and Burton spent 99 days drifting on the ice, but in the end they were rescued. Their journey took nearly three years.

▶ A Sno-Cat vehicle perched dangerously across a crevasse during the 1957 Trans-Antarctic expedition. The Sno-Cats have crevasse detectors but these did not always warn them of the danger ahead.

New challenges

▲ Ranulph Fiennes and Charles Burton leave Borga for their 3520 km crossing of Antarctica. This was the only crossing made in open vehicles. It was also the longest crossing of the frozen continent ever made.

▲ Charles Burton checks out a crevasse on the Transglobe Expedition to the Antarctic. The snow bridge can be seen in front of the snowmobile. The photograph was taken by Ranulph Fiennes.

The Poles today

Today, there are more than 50 scientific bases in Antarctica. There is also an American base at the South Pole itself. No one country owns Antarctica, so any nation can carry out scientific work there.

There can be no permanent bases on the drifting ice at the North Pole, but scientists can visit the area to study the birds, animals and fish that live in the Arctic regions. In the Arctic and the Antarctic, the explorers of the past opened the way for the scientists of today.

Pathfinders
Quiz

How much can you remember about this book? Try this quiz and use the glossary and index to help you check your answers.

1. These names are back to front. Can you find five polar explorers among them?

    a) TTOCS, b) NAGAER,
    c) ENOTSGNIVIL, d) YRRAP,
    e) NESDNUMA f) NNELG,
    g) NOTELKCAHS, h) OLOP OCRAM,
    i) SUBMULOC, j) DRYB

2. Can you guess what this sentence says in full?

    'I _____ _____ _____ outside, and I _____ be _____ time'.
    Clue: It was said by a brave man giving his life to try to save his friends.

3. Match the descriptions given in (a) to (f) to the words numbered (1) to (6) below them.

    a) The coldest places on Earth
    b) An ocean ringed by land
    c) A large animal found in Arctic regions
    d) A tall floating block of ice
    e) Small boats used by the Inuit.
    f) A disease caused by not eating fresh fruit

    1) an iceberg
    2) kayaks
    3) the Arctic
    4) scurvy
    5) the Poles
    6) polar bear

4. Put the following events in the order they took place.

    a) Scott's last journey
    b) The first Trans-Antarctic crossing
    c) The first flight over the North Pole
    d) The first voyage through the Northwest Passage
    e) Franklin's last expedition

5. Complete the following sentences with (a), (b), (c) or (d):

    1) Dogs used for hauling sledges in polar regions are called
        a) hounds.
        b) moose.
        c) caribou.
        d) huskies.

    2) Splits in the ice which lead to dangerous falls are
        a) crevasses.
        b) cliffs.
        c) glaciers.
        d) tunnels.

    3) Blizzards are
        a) birds.
        b) snowstorms.
        c) fish.
        d) a type of sledge.

    4) The South Pole is at latitude
        a) 90° south.
        b) 100° south.
        c) 90° north.
        d) 0°.

Quiz

5) In 1914, Shackleton and his men were stopped by
   a) storms.
   b) icebergs.
   c) whales.
   d) pack ice.

6) A snowmobile is a
   a) game played by the Inuit.
   b) a type of boat.
   c) a way of getting down icy slopes.
   d) a motor sledge.

6. How many polar explorers can you find with names beginning with P or S?

7. Which polar region is:
   a) nearest to Baffin Island?
   b) coldest in June?
   c) about one-tenth of the Earth's surface?
   d) inhabited by a small number of scientists?
   e) inside the Arctic Circle?

8. Who or what
   a) shows which direction is north?
   b) have lived in Arctic regions for thousands of years?
   c) was abandoned by his crew in a small boat?
   d) tied a boat to an iceberg?
   e) left Norway in a hurry because he owed money?

9. Are these statements true or false?
   a) The polar region in the north is called the Antarctic.
   b) The magnetic south is the true south.
   c) The route from the Atlantic Ocean to the Pacific Ocean around the north of Canada is the Northwest Passage.
   d) Amundsen was a poor skier.
   e) Greenland is an island.

Answers

1. a) SCOTT, b) LIVINGSTONE, c) PARRY, d) AMUNDSEN, e) GLENN, f) SHACKLETON, g) MARCO POLO, h) COLUMBUS, i) BYRD
2. "I am just going outside and I may be some time." Lawrence Oates.
3. (a) 5, (b) 3, (c) 6, (d) 1, (e) 2, (f) 4
4. (e), (d), (a), (c), (b)
5. 1 (d), 2 (a), 3 (b), 4 (a), 5 (d), 6 (d)
6. Parry, Peary, Shackleton, Scott, Smith
7. (a) North, (b) South, (c) South, (d) South, (e) North
8. (a) a compass, (b) Inuit and Saami, (c) Hudson, (d) Parry, (e) Amundsen
9. (a) false, (b) false, (c) true, (d) false, (e) true

45

Pathfinders

Glossary

advance party: a group of people in an expedition who are sent ahead. They may take supplies to leave along the route for the main party following behind. They may also see if the route is suitable

Antarctic: the region south of the Antarctic Circle around the South Pole. Most of it is a huge land mass which is covered in snow and ice

Antarctic Circle: an imaginary circle around the Earth which is parallel to the Equator. This circle is found at latitude 66° 32′ S

Arctic: the region north of the Arctic Circle around the North Pole. Most of the area is frozen sea. This is a very cold region

Arctic Circle: an imaginary circle around the Earth which is parallel to the Equator. This circle is found at latitude 66° 32′ N

base: a place from which an organization or expedition works. It will keep its main supplies at the base

blizzard: a snowstorm blown by a very strong, very cold wind

compass: an instrument that is used to find direction. It contains a needle which points north. The four points of the compass are N (north), S (south), E (east), W (west)

continent: a large mass of land, sometimes including many countries. The Earth is divided into seven continents

crevasse: a deep split in a mass of ice or snow

crew: the group of people who work together on a ship or plane

degrees: the unit of measurement of an angle. If you turn right around once when you are standing on the ground, you will turn 360 degrees

drift: to be carried by air or wind without any means of steering

Equator: an imaginary circle around the middle of the Earth. The hottest parts of the world are nearest the Equator

expedition: an organized journey which is made for a special purpose. Explorers went on expeditions to find out about new lands

experiment: a test to try out an idea. People carry out experiments when they want to find out about something

frostbite: damage to the body, usually fingers, ears, toes and nose. This is caused by severe cold

glacier: a slow-moving river of ice

husky dogs: a breed of dog which can live in the polar regions. This dog has a thick coat to protect it from the cold

iceberg: a large piece of ice which floats like an island in the sea. Most of the ice is under the surface of the sea

ice pack: a vast area of floating ice that has been driven together by winds and currents

ice shelf: a thick block of ice which is attached to land. It covers a large area of sea and floats on it

invention: something that has not been thought of or made before

kayak: a small, light boat made of sealskin

latitude: one of many imaginary lines drawn around the world from east to west and above or below the Equator. A position on the Earth north or south of the Equator

Glossary

launch: to start something moving. To put a ship into water

magnetic north: The North Magnetic Pole is the direction in which a compass needle points. This is not the same as the true north, which is the North Pole. The magnetic poles move with the tilting of the Earth

magnetic south: the opposite direction to the North Magnetic Pole which is shown on a compass. This is not the true south, which is the South Pole. The magnetic poles move with the tilting of the Earth

mountain range: a line of mountains

Northwest Passage: a passage for ships along the northern coast of America. Explorers searched for this route from the Atlantic Ocean to the Pacific Ocean as a way through to the continent of Asia

pack ice: a large area of floating ice that drifts around in the sea. It sometimes breaks into smaller pieces

permafrost: soil beneath the surface of the ground that is frozen all the time

plateau: a large area of high, flat land

polar region: either of the parts of the world which are found close to the South Pole or the North Pole

route: the way to get from one place to another. Routes are shown on maps and plans

scurvy: a disease caused by lack of vitamin C. This vitamin can be found in fresh fruit and vegetables. The disease leads to bleeding of the gums and damage to the teeth and bones of the body

snowmobile: a small vehicle designed to travel over ice and snow. It has skis instead of wheels

supplies: food, fuel or equipment needed for an expedition or a trip

support group: a group of people who give help and support to the main party on an expedition

thaw: to raise the temperature of something above its freezing point, so it becomes liquid. When ice thaws, it becomes water

whaling station: a place where people who fish for whales live and deal with the whales they have caught

Index

A
Adélie Land 25
Alaska, US 7, 17, 41
Amundsen, Roald 16, 17, 21, 30, 32, 34, 35, 40, 41, 42
Anchorage, Alaska 7
Antarctic 4, 5, 22, 23, 24, 25, 26, 27, 28, 30, 38, 40, 42, 43
Antarctica 4, 5, 22, 23, 24, 25, 26, 27, 28, 30, 38, 41, 42, 43
Antarctic Circle 6, 22, 23, 24
Arctic 4, 5, 6, 7, 9, 10, 12, 15, 16, 17, 18, 40, 43
Arctic Circle 6, 7, 19, 22
Arctic Ocean 5, 7, 8, 12, 13, 17
Asia 8
Atlantic Ocean 8, 9
Australia 6

B
Back River 11
Baffin Island 9
Baffin, William 9
Bay of Whales 32
Beardmore Glacier 29, 33
Bennett, Floyd 40
Bowers, Lieutenant 31
Britain 6, 11, 26, 28, 30
Burton, Charles 42, 43
Byrd, Richard 40, 41, 42

C
Canada 7, 8, 17
Cape of Good Hope 8
Cherry-Garrard, Apsley 31
Cook, Frederick 19, 21
Cook, James 23, 24

D
De Long, George 13
Discovery, the 26, 27
d'Urville, Jules 25

E
Elephant Island 39
Ellesmere Island 19
Ellsworth, Lincoln 40
Endurance, the 38, 39
Equator 6, 21
Erebus, the 10
Europe 8, 24
Evans, Edgar 35, 36

F
Fiennes, Ranulph 5, 42, 43
Floyd Bennett, the 41
Fox, the 11
Fram, the 13, 14, 15, 21, 30, 32
France 25
Franklin, John 10, 11, 16
Franz Josef Land 14
Frobisher, Martin 8, 9
Fuchs, Vivian 42

G
Great Lakes 8
Great Slave Lake 10
Greenland 7, 8, 13, 18
Gjöa, the 17
Griper, the 9

H
Hecla, the 9
Henson, Matthew 20, 21
Hillary, Edmund 42
Hudson Bay 9, 10
Hudson, Henry 9

I
Inuit people 6, 7, 11, 13, 17, 18, 20
Italia, the 40

J
Jeannette, the 13
Johansen, Hjalmar 14, 15

K
King William Island 11

L
Lancaster Sound 9, 10
latitude 6
Little America 41
London, Britain 6

M
Maori people 23
magnetic north 7
magnetic south 7, 29
Markham 26
Melville Island 9
Mount Erebus 28
Murmansk 7

N
Nansen, Fridtjof 13, 14, 15, 16, 42
Nelson River 10
New Siberian Islands 13, 14
New York, US 6
New Zealand 23, 25
Nimrod, the 28, 29
Nobile, Umberto 40
Norge, the 40
North America 8
North Pole 4, 5, 6, 7, 12, 13, 14, 15, 16, 18, 19, 20, 21, 30, 40, 42, 43
Northwest Passage 8, 9, 10, 12, 16, 17
Norway 13, 15, 16, 17, 21, 35, 40

O
Oates, Lawrence 35, 36
Ocean Camp 38

P
Pacific Ocean 8, 9, 17, 23
Parry, William Edward 9, 12
Peary, Jo 18
Peary, Robert 18, 19, 20, 21, 30, 42

R
Rae, Dr John 11
Resolution, the 23
Roosevelt, the 19, 20, 21
Roosevelt, President Theodore 19
Ross Ice Shelf 25, 27, 29, 34, 36, 37, 41
Ross, James 25, 26
Ross Sea 42

S
Saami people 7
Scott, Robert 26, 27, 28, 29, 30, 31, 32, 33, 34, 35, 36, 37, 41, 42
Shackleton, Ernest 26, 28, 29, 30, 35, 38, 39, 42
Siberia 13, 19
Smith, William 24
Sno-Cat 42
snowmobile 42, 43
South America 8, 9
South Georgia 39
South Pole 4, 5, 6, 7, 21, 22, 29, 30, 31, 32, 33, 34, 35, 38, 40, 41, 42, 43
South Shetland Islands 24
St Lawrence River 8
Sydney, Australia 6

T
Terra Nova, the 30, 31
Terror, the 10
Transglobe Expedition 5, 23, 43

U
United States 6, 7, 17, 18, 19, 21, 24, 25, 41
USSR 7

W
Weddell Sea 38, 42
Wilkes, Charles 24, 25
Wilson, Edward 30, 31, 36, 37
Windward, the 19